Tattered Legacy

Cindy Mohnen Tharp

Trilogy Christian Publishers
A Wholly Owned Subsidary of Trinity Broadcasting Network
2442 Michelle Drive
Tustin, CA 92780

For information, address Trilogy Christian Publishing
Rights Department, 2442 Michelle Drive, Tustin, Ca 92780.
Trilogy Christian Publishing/ TBN and colophon are trademarks
of Trinity Broadcasting Network.
For information about special discounts for bulk purchases, please
contact Trilogy Christian Publishing.
Manufactured in the United States of America

10 9 8 7 6 5 4 3 2 1
Library of Congress Cataloging-in-Publication Data is available.
ISBN 978-1-64088-271-3
ISBN 978-1-64088-272-0

To my mother, who lived her ninety-four-year legacy with quiet determination,
all the while holding on to the hand of Jesus.

Acknowledgments

There is a saying that no man is an island, and that is so true for this devotional. I literally could not have completed it without the help of some very important people. First, my mother, Vera Mohnen, who is the reason for every page written. Thank you so much Mom, for living the life you did, in the way you did, for so many years. And thank you for leaving a quiet legacy that I only discovered after you went to live with Jesus. Secondly, my father, Lawrence (Bud) Mohnen, who gave me his blessing from the start, and was a vital part of the whole process. Thank you for your love and encouragement every step of the way. Your supportive words kept me going!

Additionally, I want to thank my sisters, Karen Clausen and Lexie Caraway, who, with maybe a bit of breath-holding, believed in their little sister and supported me, anyway. I can't believe how blessed I am to have the sisters that I do. Then a thank you to my husband, Don Tharp, who happily spent many hours after coming home from work to read and re-read the numerous drafts of this book. I love you, and I am blessed that you're my husband. Next, I want to thank my children, Amber Rankin and Desira Adams, who were excited for me to accomplish the task at hand and rallied around me. I am blessed to have the children that I do. I am so proud of you both!

A shout out goes to my mother-in-law and father-in-law, Don and Betty Tharp, who were willing to support this idea, and in a very big way helped to move it along. Thank you for taking a chance on me, and thank you for being who you are. Also, those at Trilogy: Acquisitions Executive, Mark Mingle, who answered so many questions with much patience. You were so supportive! Project Manager Melissa Miller, who kept me up-to-date on where the production process was and was so sweet in doing so. Editor Shelley Jobe, who cared for my book as if it were her own, and whose kind but con-

Acknowledgments

structive advice was invaluable, and Designer Kaycee Tattershall, who masterminded the design and layout of the book. Lastly, thank you to my friends who supported me during the process by staying positive about something they didn't know if I could handle or not! You're the best.

Table of Contents

A Legacy Discovered

I have a few of my mother's belongings in my home: a scarf that still has the aroma of her White Rain hair spray on it, some blankets that she used every day as she slept in her chair, and a few articles of clothing, one of which she often wore at home when she got chilled. I can actually see a picture in my mind of her putting the soft, light blue jacket on as I put my arms through the sleeves.

The most cherished belonging I have of hers is a well-loved but tattered Amplified version of the Bible. It's so worn that the binding has been re-built throughout the years in various types and layers of tape to keep it half-way intact. The pages are rippled, yellowed with age, and the edges are raw from use. The plastic book tabs are brittle and some have broken apart. Every so often, when I turn the pages, a fleeting scent of her hand lotion rises to my nose, and the cover's original color has given way to a lighter undercoat where her hands held it day after day. I love to put my hands where hers were as if it would bring me close to her again somehow, and some days I would find myself wondering out loud why she underlined or made note of a verse, wishing I could hear her voice in the answer.

I had no idea that my quiet time within these pages would actually be a legacy from my mom, and that the hand-written notes and underlined verses would be a reminder of what's really important.

All of us have a legacy to share, no matter the shape of it. It can happen so quietly (as in my mother's case) that we don't even realize we are building blocks to stand on for those that go behind us.

Although Mom studied every book in her Bible, I have chosen a few underlined verses and hand-written notes that I believe are good examples for us to think about as we learn to live our lives well. The scripture quotes, although in older verbiage, have been kept true to the old Amplified Bible Mom was using, copyright 1965. However, I have also added a newer bible version (The New International Version) for some scripture quotes to aid in the understanding of the scripture.

Thanks for joining in the journey. I'm so glad you're here! Be blessed!

Woven Together

For we are God's [own] handiwork, (His workmanship), rec-
reated in Christ Jesus, [born anew] that we may do those
good works which God predestined (planned beforehand) for
us, (taking paths which He prepared ahead of time) that we
should walk in them—living the good life which He prear-
ranged and made ready for us to live.

(Ephesians 2:10, AMPC)

As I began my journey through my mother's Bible, I decided I would just take a few pages per day to see what was important to her. Then one day, I noticed that something was inside; I flipped to that page and found a crocheted cross done by my mother's own hand. It took my breath away as any unexpected reminder of a loved one would. This blue and white cross was hand-crafted in tiny stitches, which I had seen before in little dresses that Mom made for myself and my sisters when we were babies. Honestly, I have no idea how she crocheted so small! We are talking T.I.N.Y.! The blue has held its color, but the white appears to be a bit "tea-stained" with age.

The scripture above is about being made new in Christ so that we can live out our purpose in Him. I think Mom's crocheted cross is a good illustration of that. The final product came from a ball of yarn that didn't look anything like a cross. Mom selected a specific crochet pattern to turn that yarn into something useful and meaningful. She knew what the yarn was going to be before it was finished. Each stitch was linked to the next stitch, and the next, until it was complete. Then the cross served its purpose as a bookmark— all because of a bunch of fibers deliberately twisted together.

Can you just envision God creating us to serve our purposes? "Crocheting" us together, one stitch at a time, using His pattern, and being deliberate about the final product and how it would be used? In our fast-paced world, sometimes it's difficult to find what our purpose is. Sometimes we look to the world for an answer—which eventually comes up void. But if we take the time to understand where God is leading us, it will save us a lot of energy and frustration in our busy lives.

Your Legacy…

Do you know what your purpose is? Write down three examples of how God has used you in specific ways for the benefit of others. Really. Just do it. Seeing it on paper will remind you of how God made you and give you confidence for future endeavors to help others!

_____

_____

_____

_____

I'm Supposed to Be Happy When?

Consider it wholly joyful, my brethren, whenever you are enveloped in or encounter trials of any sort, or fall into various temptations. Be assured and understand that the trial and proving of your faith bring out endurance and steadfastness and patience. But let endurance and steadfastness and patience have full play and do a thorough work, so that you may be [people] perfectly and fully developed (with no defects), lacking nothing.

(James 1:2-4, AMPC)

Consider it pure joy, my brothers, whenever you face trials of many kinds, because you know that the testing of your faith develops perseverance. Perseverance must finish its work so that you may be mature and complete, not lacking anything.

(James 1:2-4, NIV)

First of all, I want to say, "Mom, did you *have* to underline this one?" I don't know about you, my friend, but I really don't like trials! So why in the world should we consider challenges in our lives to be something that produces good? After all, pain resides there! But my mother knew a thing or two about enduring long-term health challenges, and she did so with as much grace as anyone could. She must have known this scripture to be true, and that gives me hope.

If you are going through a challenge right now, you may be thinking, *This is crazy! I don't feel like I can endure, I'm not steadfast, and I'm sure not patient! And who cares about lacking nothing and being perfectly developed when it's all I can do to get through each day!* Can I just say, "I know how you feel?" I've had trials where I wasn't sure if I would make it through another day. Where just breathing in and out took

5

most of my energy. It can be hard!

When we try to get through a trial on our terms, many times we get angry, depressed, anxious, and even get stuck in the issue, thinking there's no way out. But when we link arms with God, it makes all the difference. And have you noticed that, after our trials are over and we've made it through, we are more patient, can endure more easily, and are more steadfast when the next challenge comes our way? In fact, we're even able to help others through the same challenge. That wouldn't have happened if we hadn't gone through the first trial, to begin with. It's like we have to practice, to be able to handle life's ups and downs. And, like anything else, with practice comes confidence to move forward the next time.

I know it's never nice to go through a tough time. It can be heart-rending. But hang in there, my friend. You are not alone, and you will get through it!

Your Legacy...
Write down one challenge you've come through with more patience and endurance. Putting it in writing will help you remember how you made it through the trial. You'll be able to refer back to it when the next trial comes, and that reminder will help take the fear out of future obstacles!

_____

_____

_____

_____

Take My Vitals, Please

For the Lord searches all hearts and minds, and understands all the wandering of the thoughts. If you seek Him—inquiring for and of Him, and requiring Him as your first and vital necessity—you will find Him; but if you forsake Him, He will cast you off forever!

(1 Chronicles 28: Last half of verse 9, AMPC)

...for the LORD searches every heart and understands every motive behind the thoughts. If you seek him, he will be found by you; but if you forsake him, he will reject you forever.

(1 Chronicles 28: Last half of verse 9, NIV)

This verse is a small part of a discussion between God, David, and Solomon, regarding who was to build a house for the Ark of the Covenant. But what I want you to notice is the particular wording in this Amplified version, "requiring Him as your first and vital necessity." David was telling his son, Solomon, that he needed to have a significant, life-relevant, relationship with God.

Finding this verse underlined did not surprise me. But it made me think, and I had to ask myself if God was a vital part of my own life. When something is vital to us, it means that we cannot live without it; it is imperative to our livelihood. Here's how the Merriam-Webster Dictionary defines the word vital: "Of the utmost importance; fundamentally concerned with or affecting life or living beings; concerned with or necessary to the maintenance of life" (Merriam-Webster 2019). Wow!

Do I find God *vital* to my existence? Would I feel a real sense of void if I didn't have Him in my life every day? Is He as necessary

7

as the very air I breathe and the heart that beats inside my chest—and (dare I say it)—my cell phone? (Joking, of course, or maybe not!) That's a powerful question!

Your Legacy...
If you had to choose between having your cell phone with you all day and feeling God's presence all day, which would you choose? Why?

_____

_____

_____

_____

What Do You Want?

That night God appeared to Solomon and said to him, Ask what I shall give you.

(2 Chronicles 1:7, AMPC)

Give me now wisdom and knowledge to go out and come in before this people; for who can rule this Your people, that is so great?

(2 Chronicles 1:10, AMPC)

What would you ask for if God granted you something? Your house paid off? A new car? Free groceries for a year? Solomon was a king. He could have asked God for gold and rubies. Instead, he asked for wisdom and knowledge so that he could lead his people. It's such a good reminder to me of what's really important. Cars and other material items come and go. But wisdom and knowledge will take us throughout our lives, helping us to discern right from wrong, what relationships we should be a part of (or not!), and how to manage our finances, etc. With God's wisdom, we can choose wisely, and the knowledge will help us make sound decisions.

So, thanks Mom, for bringing this to my attention. Solomon was very smart in asking God for the two things that cover most things in life!

Your Legacy...

Ask your family members what they would want if God granted them something. This is a great way to bring to light what's really important!

What Do You Want?

_____

_____

_____

_____

Tears

Jesus wept.

(John 11:35, AMPC)

There is a joke that if you're asked to memorize one scripture of your choice, request John 11:35. Why? Because there are only two words in it! I'm smiling as I think of that. But then the realization of the content of those two words set in, and I wondered why these words of Jesus were so important to my mother—so much so that she underlined it several times!

Was it because Jesus felt deep sorrow when a man he loved as a brother (Lazarus) died? Was it because Jesus had deep feelings even though he was Lord and Savior and did miracles? Was it because if Jesus cried, it's ok for us to cry, too? Maybe it was knowing that if Jesus cried for his friend, he also cries for us when we hurt. And when we think of Jesus in that way, he's no longer some invisible force that may or may not hear us when we cry out as well. It's quite possible that this verse was important to my mother because she had a family of her own, and what mother doesn't shed a tear or two over her children? Whatever it was, I'm thankful to think about Jesus as someone who truly cares for us enough to shed real, deep, heartfelt tears.

Your Legacy...
Does it help to know that "Jesus wept"? Does it make Him real to you? Does it give you a sense of peace that you are not alone when you're sad?

_____

_____

_____

_____

Persistent Faith

Now faith is the assurance (the confirmation, the title-deed)
of the things [we] hope for, being the proof of things [we] do
not see and the conviction of their reality—faith perceiving as
real fact what is not revealed to the senses.

(Hebrews 11:1, AMPC)

Sometimes it's just one word that can make all the difference in how we understand the information we're given. In this case, the word "is" had parentheses around it, and next to that little two-letter word Mom wrote "present tense." Mom could have missed this all-important word "is," but I'm so glad she didn't!

Isn't it wonderful that this verse does not say faith "was" being sure of what we hope for. It's not past tense. Instead, it's written in a current, ongoing tense that tells us we can have the type of faith that is sure and certain every day of our lives. I'm so glad we have that assurance!

Your Legacy…
How does this one word change the way you understand faith?

_____

_____

_____

_____

What Did You Say?

Out of the same mouth come forth blessing and cursing. These things, my brethren, ought not to be so.

(James 3:10, AMPC)

Oh boy! The mouth. It's so hard to control sometimes, isn't it? Maybe you feel good about everything you say. As for me, I know that I don't always talk the way I should!

As we go about our daily routines, what would happen if we remembered that God hears what comes out of our mouths? Would we be embarrassed or at peace? For me, sometimes it's hard to get through one day without getting a bit negative about a trivial matter. For instance, it's hard when someone cuts me off in traffic. At that moment, I am not thinking of positive words! However, if I would stop and think about Jesus sitting next to me in the passenger seat, you can bet I'd be more careful about what I said! Actually, He *is* there, whether I can physically see Him or not!

Your Legacy...
As you go about your day today, envision Jesus right by your side every step of the way. Then record how that affected your words.

_____

_____

_____

_____

Just Listen!

Blessed—happy, fortunate, [to be envied]—is the man whom You discipline and instruct, O Lord, and teach out of Your law; That You may give him power to hold himself calm in the days of adversity, until the [inevitable] pit of corruption is dug for the wicked.

(Psalm 94:12–13, AMPC)

Blessed is the man you discipline, O LORD, the man you teach from your law; you grant him relief from days of trouble, till a pit is dug for the wicked.

(Psalm 94:12–13, NIV)

Can you remember a time when your parents disciplined you? As I'm typing today's devotion, I'm remembering a time when my sisters were outside in the back yard climbing the neighbor's tree, which they weren't supposed to be doing. Somehow, Mom became aware of their antics (as only mothers can do) and marched outside. She found a long stick on the ground, walked toward them waving the stick in the air so that it made a swishing sound, and said, "Just listen to this!" You can bet they knew their back-sides were about to feel some trouble! But just as she said those words, the stick broke in half! Mom just stood there—stunned—at what had happened. Of course, my sisters looked on, not daring to say a word… silence dripping in the air. Obviously, all semblance of trying to look like she was in charge went out the door at that moment, and suddenly my sisters started laughing, then (fortunately) Mom joined in.

This story is so funny to me because I can't remember a time when I was ever disciplined with a branch. What a great memory that has been throughout the years, and we often teased her about it.

So, why are we blessed when God disciplines us? Because He loves us and wants the best for us! Just as our parents did when we were growing up, and like we have done with our children. God wouldn't bother with disciplining us if he didn't care or love us. We are blessed!

Your Legacy...
Can you think of a time you were disciplined? Looking back, can you say that you were blessed to be corrected? Why?

_____

_____

_____

_____

Love Never Goes Out of Style

Love never fails—never fades out or becomes obsolete or comes to an end.

(1 Corinthians 13:8, AMPC)

There are seven verse references written in the back of this Bible. I was looking at that today and decided to look inside the pages to see what one of those verses—1 Corinthians 13:8—said. This verse is part of what is called the "love chapter" in the Bible. It must've been important enough to Mom that she not only underlined it, but she wrote it in a special spot on the inside of the back cover.

Love never fails or comes to an end. I'm so thankful for that! My mother loved us three girls for seventy-one of her ninety-four years here on Earth. That's a lot of love! That type of love is not "surface" love. It's commitment. It means loving even when you don't feel like it. It's believing the best in someone when they don't even believe in themselves. And sometimes, it's just plain work! This type of love is possible when we walk hand-in-hand with the Lord, but very hard to do on our own.

What a legacy to have and what a lesson to us girls!

Your Legacy…
If you can, sit down and talk with someone who has had a long-term, healthy relationship. Ask them how they did it and think about how you can implement some ideas they may give you.

_____

_____

Love Never Goes Out of Style

_____

_____

Peace

Peace I leave with you; My [own] peace I now give and be-
queath to you.

(John 14:27, AMPC)

What would you do for some real peace? The kind of peace that covers your heart, mind, and soul with a soft, warm blanket? I'm sure if we could all go to the store and take some peace off the shelf, we would be willing to pay almost anything for it! But that's not how the Holy Spirit works.

My little mother had numerous health issues in the last part of her life on Earth. In spite of it all, my father says she never complained. She hurt in so many ways. She could have been angry and bitter, and yet, she spent time with God through it all and found that inner peace we all long for. Did she get tired of hurting? Sure, who wouldn't! But the difference is that she didn't rely on her strength to get through it. I know this for a fact because, humanly speaking, when we are in constant pain, and our bodies are not working properly, we are not naturally joyful. We complain because we hurt, and we're tired of hurting. And sometimes we get angry with God. Mom may have gotten upset and frustrated with her body, but never did I hear her ask why she was suffering. And never did she lose that connection with God.

Your Legacy...
Are you hurting? My heart truly goes out to you. I know it may seem impossible at times, but try not to dwell on the pain. Mark your calendar so that you spend time with God every day. Don't rush this. Sit in His peace. Leave your cell phone in another room and turned off. Turn on

some quiet music. Whatever it takes to get one-on-one time with the only One who can give His peace to you, "Not as the world gives," as John 14:27 says, but only as He can.

Let's Eat!

There is not one [even] one thing outside a man which by going into him can pollute and defile him, but the things which come out of a man are what defile him and make him unhallowed and unclean.

(Mark 7:15, AMPC)

Since it does not reach and enter his heart but [only his] digestive tract, and so passes on (into the place designed to receive waste)? Thus, He was making and declaring all foods (ceremonially) clean [that is, abolishing the ceremonial distinctions of the Leviticus Law].

(Mark 7:19, AMPC)

Right now, you may be thinking that this scripture is telling us we can eat anything even if it's bad for us. In reality, Jesus was talking to the Pharisees about how they were more concerned about the eating practices in the Levitical Law than the condition of their hearts. They loved the rules and regulations, but what came out of their hearts was not good, and Jesus considered it to be "unclean."

While there is a definite lesson in this scripture regarding our hearts vs. being legalistic, do you want to know what these verses made me think of? Whipped cream.

My mother *loved* whipped cream. When it was time for dessert, she would take that can of whipped cream, press the nozzle (Can you hear the airy sound it makes?), then press it some more, and then maybe some more—all with a little twinkle in her eyes. It was one of her greatest pleasures later in life. In fact, we would joke with her and tell her that she would probably take a bath in it if she could! To that, she would just look at us and grin. To this day, when

I see a can of the sweet white cream, I think of Mom, and it makes me smile. Her heart was clean, and her taste buds were sweet!

Your Legacy...

What memories do you have of a loved one? Take time to pass those happy thoughts to your family. Don't let them fade away! If you can, make a video of the special moments in your own life to pass on to your children. I have one of my parents. It's so good to have!

_____

_____

_____

_____

Prepare for Your Miracle

Then He commanded the people all to recline on the green grass by companies. So they threw themselves down in ranks in hundreds and fifties—with the regularity of arrangement of beds of herbs, looking like so many garden plots. And taking the five loaves and two fish, He looked up to heaven, and praising God gave thanks, and broke the loaves, and kept on giving them to the disciples to set before the people; and He [also] divided the two fish among [them] all. And they all ate and were satisfied. And they took up twelve [small hand] baskets full of broken pieces [from the loaves] and of the fish. And those who ate the loaves were 5,000 men.

(Mark 6:39-44, AMPC)

In these verses, Jesus was instructing his disciples to feed 5,000 men (That number did not include women and children!) that had followed Him to hear His word. The disciples didn't understand how this could be possible because they only had five loaves of bread and two fish between them. To the human mind, this was impossible!

There are five hand-written notes, of Mom's, woven around these verses:

1. "Prepare for your miracle" (a reference to verses 39 and 40).
2. "Thank God for what you've got" (verse 41).
3. "Give what you have" (verse 41).
4. "The miracle" (verse 42).
5. "Running over" (verse 43).

What a wonderful way to look at how Jesus helps us with our impossibilities! Let's take a closer look. The first note conveys that we listen to God and do what He tells us to do. The second says, be thankful for what you do have, in spite of everything. The third says, even though it may not seem like much, give what you have. Fourthly, experience the miracle that God provides. And the fifth note, be amazed at how you were not only provided for but had been given more than you needed to accomplish the task!

At one time, we lived in a very small community. We loved it there. But the kids in town didn't have a defined, positive place for them to go after school (a youth center). It was an issue that needed to be addressed, but I wasn't the one to take care of it—or so I thought. However, God had other ideas.

I finally got tired of fighting God about it and told Him that if he provided the place, I would manage the youth center. Of course, I thought I was off the hook because who would offer a building, free of charge? So, one day I walked into the office of a man who owned a building in town that was vacant. I said, "I don't have any money to pay rent on the building, but I have the time to put into managing a youth center." I still shake my head when I remember his answer. "Well, I've got the building. But I don't have the time, and I've been wondering what we could do to help the kids in town." I'd like to tell you that I jumped up and down with joy, but in reality, my next thought was, *What have I done?* I know, pretty sad, huh? And that's how Diversions Youth Center was born. It lived on even after we moved, thanks to Michelle, an awesome friend and volunteer who put her time into it.

I love the insight my mother provided here. How many times do we not follow through, don't give thanks, and don't give what we have? So, don't despair today if you think you'll never meet your goal. Give it to God, receive the blessing—and be open to what He has in store for you to do!

Your Legacy...
Write down one challenge you have today and ask God to help you. Then listen, follow His lead, and record what happens in the days to come. It's pretty amazing how God puts our steps together, in only a way He could!

_____

_____

_____

_____

What Is Love?

Love is patient, love is kind. It does not envy, it does not boast, it is not proud. It is not rude, it is not self-seeking, it is not easily angered, it keeps no record of wrongs. Love does not delight in evil but rejoices with the truth. It always protects, always trusts, always hopes, always perseveres.

(1 Corinthians 13: 4-7, NIV)

I found a hand-written note hidden away in the pages of Mom's Bible. The verses she wrote out are a well-known explanation of what love is and are found in 1 Corinthians 13:4-7. It's not easy to follow all of these descriptors. I know, I have broken them all at one time or another (more than once) and as long as I'm alive, I'll fail again! Isn't it good to know that God is full of grace?

Usually, when we write something down in long-hand, we really want to remember it, don't we? Afterward, we may post it on our refrigerator, put it in a book as Mom did, or use a sticky note and press it onto our make-up mirrors. We want to see it on a regular basis to help us grow in a certain area.

Mom also circled, "it keeps no record of wrongs." Whether someone sends us an unwelcome text on our cell phone, or there is a larger issue, the longer we live, the more we have to forgive, don't we?

You know, Mom was ninety-four when she went to live with Jesus, so I'm sure she knew a thing or two about forgiveness! And one more thing. There was a blank piece of paper with the hand-written note. Mom must have put it there so she could write more. Now, I believe it's there for me to write these same verses down. They're good ones to put into practice, aren't they?

Your Legacy...
What is it that you need to write out by hand and apply throughout your life? Take time to do that this week, then post it somewhere so you can see it often.

Our Words Matter

In the beginning God (prepared, formed, fashioned,) and cre-
ated the heavens and the earth [Hebrews 11:3.]. The earth
was without form and an empty waste, and darkness was
upon the face of the very great deep. The Spirit of God was
moving, (hovering, brooding) over the face of the waters. And
God said, Let there be light; and there was light.

(Genesis 1:1-3, AMPC)

Did you know that throughout this first chapter of Genesis, the words "God said" are printed nine times? It was easy to count because every one was underlined. The first chapter in Genesis is telling us how God formed the earth and everything that became part of it. The verses do not say, "God waved his hand," or "God nodded his head" and it was done. They say God *said*. Why is this so important to you and me?

While we are not God and do not have some magical power to change the sky from blue to green, we do have the power to uplift and mold those around us by what we say. For instance, when our children flunk a test, do we say, "What is wrong with you?" or do we say, "I'm sorry this test was hard for you, but I bet you can figure it out and ace it next time."

Here's another example. When we notice a friend's new haircut, do we say, "Hey, that haircut looks great on you!" Or, do we refuse to say anything at all because we've had a bad day and don't feel like giving a compliment? If someone comes to us with a challenge they're facing, do we tell them to get over it, or do we tell them that we believe in them and know they can get through it?

How about when we're standing in line at the store, and we look at the cashier who appears to have no energy left for the day but is doing the best they can. You'll be surprised how much their countenance changes when you treat them as someone who is doing you a service! The whole point is to speak life to someone because uplifting words help a person move forward. We all need that, don't we?

Your Legacy...
Who can you speak life into today? Be deliberate. Don't hesitate. Just do it. You'll both be blessed when you do!

_____

_____

_____

_____

He's Got Your Back

The Lord will fight for you, and you shall hold your peace and remain at rest.

(Exodus 14:14, AMPC)

Sometimes an underlined verse in Mom's Bible was also underlined in mine. And this is one of them. It's one of my favorite verses because it says that God has my back! When I get anxious about something in the future that I can't control (Life is *full* of those, isn't it?), this is my go to verse.

Chapter 14 in Exodus tells us the familiar story of Moses and the Israelites, Pharaoh and the Egyptians and the famous parting of the waters so that Moses and the Israelites could cross to safety. It's so full of imagery that I highly recommend you grab your Bible and read the chapter. Most of us have the Hollywood version of this in our minds, but it's best to find all the details straight from God. In a nutshell, Moses and the Israelites were running from Pharaoh and the Egyptians because Pharaoh wanted to enslave the Israelites once again. Moses and the Israelites came to a body of water, which they could not cross on their own. They thought they were trapped. Enter God! God instructed Moses to stretch out his hand over the sea, the waters parted, and they fled to safety on dry ground. The Egyptians followed, but they all died because God caused the water to fall on them.

Now, if you're like me, you've had those moments in life where you thought you were trapped. With human eyes, you saw no way out. You've tried everything you can think of to find safety or control a situation, but it just seems hopeless. Then, at just the right moment, God enters the picture. He may not part real water for you, but He knows what needs to be done and will provide the answer. We just have to let Him and follow his lead as Moses did. Sometimes, that's the hard part, isn't it? God's answers may not look like ours at all! And then we question Him. Notice Moses didn't. He just stretched out his hand over the sea as God had told him to, and the sea parted.

Can you imagine if someone told us that all we had to do is reach our hand across something and the answer would come? I'm afraid we'd walk away shaking our heads. But Moses had faith that God would take care of them and lead them to safety, so he obeyed.

I wonder how many times I've missed God's help because I didn't listen to His voice, or just thought to myself, *Well, that's just silly!* —when He brought a solution to my attention?

Your Legacy...

Are you facing something a little scary right now? Maybe you know the next step God wants you to take, but you're afraid to do it. It's okay! Take that step. We don't have to know the full story—because God does! He's so good to give us baby steps to reach our goal so that we don't get overwhelmed with the whole.

_____

_____

_____

_____

Approval Seeking

Let the words of my mouth and the meditation of my heart be acceptable in Your sight, O Lord, my [firm, impenetrable] rock and my redeemer.

(Psalm 19:14, AMPC)

Whose approval do you seek out the most? Your parents, children, siblings, or close friends? I know that I seek approval from different people, for various reasons. And they may not always agree with me. Or maybe they're right on board with what I've said or done. But it can be a real roller coaster ride, screams included, when we seek out approval from those who are just as human as we are. I'm not saying we shouldn't include the people we love into our lives. But what I am saying is… if God is truly our solid rock, He's the one that we should sift our thoughts through first.

Your Legacy…
If you have children, who are you training them to seek approval and acceptance from first? Whom do you go to first?

_____

_____

_____

_____

Let's Go Shopping

And John wore clothing woven of camel's hair, and had a leather girdle around his loins, and ate locusts and wild honey.

(Mark 1:6, AMPC)

John wore clothing made of camel's hair, with a leather belt around his waist, and he ate locusts and wild honey.

(Mark 1:6, NIV)

You may be thinking that this was a strange scripture for my mother to put parentheses around, but I'm not in charge of what Mom made a note of. I'm just going with the flow!

This scripture is a description of what John the Baptist wore (More power to him... sounds itchy and ouch-y to me!) and ate (Again, more power to him!), but it made me think of what we wear and how it can be a powerful part of our legacy. For men and women alike—although, probably more for women—clothing is a part of our identity and can tell those around us a lot about who we are—and Whose we are. I'm not talking about the brand of clothing we wear or how much money we spend on our tops, pants, and dresses. I *am* referring to... Modesty.

Do we dress modestly, or do we take it a bit too far, showing more of ourselves than is necessary? Uh oh, did I just say that? Yep. When I was in high school in the '70s, I wore miniskirts and halter tops. That was the fashion of the day. Mom did not approve because that type of clothing showed way too much skin. And now that I look back on it, she was right.

Maybe we can take a moment and decide why we show a little more than we should. What is our goal in doing so? Is it a good goal, one that will be honoring to yourself and God?

37

Your Legacy…

As you look at the items in your closet, what would you say your "clothing legacy" would be? Give it an actual label. Does your label say, "God Approved?" If not, maybe some changes are in order. Don't be sad. It's a good reason to go shopping!

I Can See Clearly Now

Then He put His hands on his eyes again, and the man looked intently [that is, fixed his eyes on definite objects], and he was restored, and saw everything distinctly—even what was at a distance.

(Mark 8:25, AMPC)

This is an account of a blind man and Jesus, and how Jesus restored the man's eyes. I love this scripture because it says that not only was the blind man's sight restored, but "he saw everything distinctly—even what was at a distance."

Later in life, Mom had some vision problems, which caused her to see double. Thankfully, the doctor prescribed corrective lenses so she could see properly again. How wonderful that must have been for her!

So, what about you and me? Do our eyes need a bit of "adjusting?" Have the movies we've been watching dimmed our view of Jesus? How about the internet? Our texts? The list goes on. What our eyes see goes straight to the mind and heart. And if we continue to look at things that are not helpful, our souls can become dimmed to Jesus. But what happens when we use Jesus as the barometer for what we put in front of our eyes? I'd say it clears our vision up pretty fast, doesn't it?

Your Legacy…
Take time today to go through your home movies, books, magazines, and the internet. Literally ask Jesus if you're looking at things that are healthy to your spiritual life. If the answer is "No," then have the courage to throw it out. Then begin to replace those items with healthier choic-

es. It's so good to see clearly, and if you have children, you won't have to worry about whether they'll find something that will have a negative effect on their life.

What's Your Name?

And Jesus went on with His disciples to the villages of Cae-
sarea Philippi, and on the way He asked His disciples, Who
do people say that I am? And they answered [Him], John the
Baptist; and others, Elijah, but others, One of the prophets.
And He asked them, But who do you yourselves say that I
am? Peter replied to Him, You are the Christ, the Messiah,
the Anointed One.

(Mark 8:27-29, AMPC)

Although the only correct name for Jesus in this scripture is in Peter's reply, He had other names as well, such as the Son of God. What names do you have? My mother had several: Mom, Mother, Wife, Vera, Grannie, Great Grandma, Grandma, Mrs., Sister, Daughter, and a pet name my dad had for her. We all have more than one name, don't we? And names do matter! They all signify an independent part of us.

As for myself, one of my coveted names is "Garan". It's special because it came out of the mouth of my first grandson when he tried to pronounce "Grandma". Those little lips just couldn't quite form around the proper name, so out came a new word, and suddenly, I had a new name! It wasn't what I thought I'd be called as a grandmother, but there it was, and he was so cute, what else could I do but announce it as official? I've been Garan ever since. And you know what? I wouldn't have it any other way!

Let's think about other names we may have. Some are nice and some not-so-much. We can begin with the names we should strive for. How about Giving, Merciful, and Patient? Or Up lifter, Trustworthy, or Forgiving? Wouldn't it be wonderful for people to give us those names? But then again, we may have names that hurt

41

others and don't work well for our own lives, either. These names may include Boastful, Angry, Self-Seeking, Negative, Hurtful, and Jealous. Ouch!

Whatever names you and I may have, I pray that we strive every day to become more of the positive and less of the negative.

Your Legacy...

First, write down a few names (attributes) that you think you have. Then, have your spouse or a close friend write down the names they would give you. Are there any surprises? Does anything match? Take the two lists and think about which attributes you would like to strengthen, and which ones are not helpful for your Christian growth. Then work on building up the positive and letting go of the negative.

_____

_____

_____

_____

Time Well Spent

*My people are destroyed for lack of knowledge; because you,
[the priestly nation] have rejected knowledge, I will also reject you, that you shall be no priest to Me; seeing you have
forgotten the law of your God, I will also forget your children.*

(Hosea 4:6, AMPC)

*My people are destroyed for lack of knowledge. Because you
have rejected knowledge, I also reject you as my priests; because you have ignored the law of your God, I also will ignore
your children.*

(Hosea 4:6, NIV)

The book of Hosea is written from God to the Israelites at a very
distinct time. They were not following what God set out for them to
do. Instead, they were following idols. In essence, they were morally
and socially corrupt. The priests of that day were just as guilty as the
people were. They were ignoring God's instruction and therefore
couldn't really love Him and have a relationship with Him. Because
of this, their lives weren't going so well. Poverty and famine kicked
in.

What is it that you want to learn the most? A game you
can play on your phone or iPad? History? Painting? We all have
something we enjoy and spend a lot of time on. And there's nothing
wrong with that. The problem comes when we spend more time on
those things than spending time with God and getting to know who
He is. So, if you feel like I'm stepping on your toes right now... no
worries, my toes are hurting too! In today's world, we have so many
things to distract us from opening and reading our Bibles, don't we?

So, why is it so important to learn about God? Well, let's back up a bit and ask why was it important to learn about your spouse? We don't generally pick someone off of a busy street and instantly get married. We need to know this person first. For instance, what are their opinions about finances and children? How do they care for their parents? We have so many questions for a future spouse! We need to know if they are a good match and believe as we do. Why? Because we are planning on putting our trust in them. That's a big commitment. In the same way, if we want a close relationship with God, we must learn about Him. Search what He says. Understand who He is. If we don't, we will not be able to have a close relationship with Him. And without that, we may be "destroyed for lack of knowledge."

Your Legacy...

What is one thing you've been spending a lot of time on that you could replace with reading God's word? TV, iPad, cell phone? There are many distractions, aren't there?

_____

_____

_____

_____

Family

But if a widow has children or grandchildren, see to it that these are first made to understand that it is their religious duty (to defray their natural obligation to those) at home, and make return to their parents or grandparents [for all their care by contributing to their maintenance], for this is acceptable in the sight of God.

(1 Timothy 5:4, AMPC)

But if a widow has children or grandchildren, these should learn first of all to put their religion into practice by caring for their own family and so repaying their parents and grandparents, for this is pleasing to God.

(1 Timothy 5:4, NIV)

What does your family look like? Five children, one parent, ten grandchildren, four dogs, and two cats? In the family I grew up in, I had two sisters and my mom and dad. After marriage, my own family became two children, and then two grandchildren (Plus two grand-guinea pigs and two grand-cats!).

My two sisters live in the same area as my mom and dad, and they are my heroes for taking such good care of Mom in her later years. My dad is also on my hero list because he quietly and lovingly took care of Mom every day. Unfortunately, I don't live in the same area at all. In fact, I'm sixteen hours away! I visit as often as I can, but I was not as pivotal in caring for my mom in the same way my sisters and father did. They loved and cared for Mom as best they could, and they did an amazing job. So, thank you, Karen, Lexie, and Dad. You are a blessing!

I am reminded that our children watch and learn how we

care for those we love, and they will pass on those learned actions to us as we get older. In other words, if we mistreat our parents, then how can we expect our children to treat us any differently? Hmm… now *that* will get our attention, won't it?

I am blessed to have grown up in a family that cares for one another. If you have not or like me, you don't live where your family does, God can bless you with others who become like family, so take hope!

Your Legacy…

Do you have parents or loved ones who need your care in some way? If so, are your actions "pleasing to God" and something that you want your children to witness? If not, what steps can you take to make the necessary changes?

_____

_____

_____

_____

Nine to Five

And whatever you do—no matter what it is—in word or deed, do everything in the name of the Lord Jesus and in [dependence upon] His Person, giving praise to God the Father through Him.

(Colossians 3:17, AMPC)

What job do you have? Whether it's accounting, an actor, or a mom working at home, we all have jobs to do. But do we do them to the best of our ability as if Jesus was our boss? Or do we shirk some duties or leave them for someone else to do? Do we take shortcuts, or do we stay the course? Do we go above and beyond, or do the least amount we are required to do?

I know if you are working in a job that may seem unimportant or you don't really enjoy, it's hard to think about working hand-in-hand with God. After all, what's the point? It doesn't really matter to anyone else, right? I disagree!

Are you a cashier? Without you, the rest of us couldn't purchase the items we need. We'd walk out the door with our items, and then end up in jail! Are you a janitor? If it weren't for you, our schools and office spaces would get filthy. Are you a garbage collector? I can't imagine what it would be like if you didn't pick up my garbage every week! Where would I put it all? And the smell... oh boy!

Sometimes, when I run into an airport bathroom (Better go one last time before the flight takes off!), the cleaning lady is also there, quietly doing a job that can't be much fun. I mean, I don't even like to clean *my* toilets (Ick–but gotta be done!), let alone hundreds that are used by strangers! It's a thankless job but very important. I try my best to thank the cleaning lady for doing a job that helps me out. And every time, without fail, her expression goes from pained to astonishment in being recognized, and then a smile. I love watching the transformation!

When my husband and I were first married, one of Don's jobs was a Street Sweeper at a theme park called Silver Dollar City in Branson, MO. He would walk the huge park with his little broom and metal dustpan on a handle, sweeping bits of trash off the streets so everyone could have a clean and pleasant place to walk—all with a smile on his face as the tourists walked by. He was able to take a job that wasn't really what he wanted to do and make it his own with a positive attitude. He knew *Whose* he was!

My mother spent seventy-one years being a great mom. I know many moms feel like they are unappreciated. But for all those years, my mother helped mold my sisters and me into who we are today. I'd say that's the most important job of all!

No matter the job, we can all do our very best, as if it were for Jesus. Are we ready to try?

Your Legacy...
While you're at work, take some time to process your job duties. Are you doing all you can? If not, how can you step it up a bit?

_____

_____

_____

_____

Not THAT Neighbor!

And He replied to him, You shall love the Lord your God with all your heart, and with all your soul, and with all your mind (intellect). [Deut. 6:5.] This is the great (most important, principal) and first commandment. And a second is like it, You shall love your neighbor as [you do] yourself [Lev.19:18.]
(Matthew 22:37-39, AMPC)

I know, I know, now I'm really meddlin'! Some days it's hard enough to love ourselves, let alone a neighbor we don't even know, or worse—someone we do and it's not a happy relationship! Ugh!

Isn't it interesting that these two commandments were the ones that Jesus responded with when the Pharisees were trying to test Him on what He thought was the greatest commandment? And it's even more astonishing when we realize that there were 613 laws (which Mom noted in the sidebar of her bible) at that time that people were expected to keep *every day* (I can't even resist chocolate for a day!). And out of those 613, Jesus told them that to love God and love your neighbor as yourself were the most important. I'm sure the Pharisees weren't too fond of what Jesus said because they were so rule oriented and had no time for the human heart and condition.

So, how are we to love our neighbor? As we love ourselves. And how do we love ourselves? Well, we make sure we buy food so we can eat. We buy ourselves clothing so that we are not naked and cold. We hang around people we love because we need that human contact. We don't sleep on a hard floor, but instead, we crawl into a nice, soft bed. In essence, we make sure that we are taken care of in every possible way for our comfort. So, how does this morph into our neighbors?

I wonder if your neighbor has had surgery, and can't drive,

49

but needs to get medications? If that were you and me, we would ask someone to drive us where we needed to go. So, why not ask if you can drive them to their destinations? Is a neighbor sick or not physically able to cook their meals? Eating is a big priority for us, isn't it? We would surely order take-out, at the very least, to make sure we were fed. So, how about fixing a meal and taking it over to your neighbor's house? Or, how about our lawns? We all like them to look nice, and it's not that much of a problem to mow it ourselves. But maybe one of your neighbors just can't mow anymore. Then what? Are you home-bound? You may not be able to run an errand for someone, but you sure can pray, and we all need that! There are so many examples of loving our neighbors as ourselves.

Let's be more aware of those around us. We'll not only bless the people in need, but we will be blessed as well!

Your Legacy...

Is there a neighbor or friend that needs help today? Reach out and suggest to them what you would like to do. Be specific. Don't ask them, "Is there anything I can do for you?" because they'll probably say no. They don't want to be a bother. But if you say, "Hi, (fill in the blank), I noticed your arm is in a cast. I'm sure it's hard for you to cook. I just made some (lasagna), and I'd love to bring some over to you. Is that ok?" If they decline, at the least they will know you care. If they accept, you'll feel so good when you're done, and it'll make their day!

Your Tribe Decides Your Vibe

I appeal to you, brethren, to be on your guard concerning those who create dissensions and difficulties and cause divisions, in opposition to the doctrine—the teaching—which you have been taught. [I warn you to turn aside from them, to] avoid them. For such persons do not serve our Lord Christ but their own appetites and base desires, and by ingratiating and flattering speech they beguile the hearts of the unsuspecting and simple-minded [people].

(Romans 16:17–18, AMPC)

I urge you, brothers, to watch out for those who cause divisions and put obstacles in your way that are contrary to the teaching you have learned. Keep away from them. For such people are not serving our Lord Christ, but their own appetites. By smooth talk and flattery they deceive the minds of naïve people.

(Romans 16:17–18, NIV)

There's a popular saying, "Your vibe attracts your tribe." That's a good saying, isn't it? In other words, your attitude attracts other people to you, whether negative or positive. But I want to turn it around and look at what happens when the group you spend time with starts dictating who you are, in essence, *"Your tribe decides your vibe."*

Whom do you spend a lot of time with—who's your "tribe?" In this letter to the Romans, Paul was trying to educate the Christians of his day and was informing them of general principles to follow in their Christian walk. This particular scripture speaks about the crowd we hang with because whomever we spend time with effects *our* actions!

When I was in high school, my parent's crowd consisted of five couples. They got together once a week at each other's homes to eat together, study the Bible together, and in general, just had fun together. There was a strong bond between them. These ten people also had children (including myself), and some of those children became good friends of mine as well. The children would gather together in a separate area of the house and have our own time together. I always felt safe and happy when we all got together. It was a positive place to be because the group members cared for one another. And that positive attitude rubbed off on me.

On the other hand, you may find yourself in a negative group. How can you tell? Do you hear a lot of gossiping? Do people in your group shove in line to be the first person to pass on a harmful "tidbit?" If someone in your group needs help, do the others respond? Are people angry all the time or play the victim card? Are you becoming more negative than positive? Take that as a clue to change who you spend time with! Don't let them drag you down a sad road. Life is too precious to waste time being negative!

Your Legacy...

Think about your friends—the people you spend the most time with. Are they the type of people that are positive, love the Lord, and truly care for you? Great! Who else can you find to bring with you to your group, someone that may need positivity in their lives? Or are the people in your group always negative and love to drag you down into their pits? If so, start looking for new ways to meet positive people. It will literally change your outlook on life.

The Donkey Said What?

And the Lord opened the mouth of the donkey, and she said to
Balaam, What have I done to you that you should strike me
these three times?

(Numbers 22:28, AMPC)

It's true. There's a story in the Bible about a talking donkey. Really.
Check it out for yourself (verses 21-33). I love that Mom included
this in her notations, and I am suddenly reminded of the time when
she won a Shetland pony. All I'll say here is: We lived in town…
Dad had to find a pasture to put it in… it was kinda wild… its name
literally was Troubles for a reason… and the man who owned the
pasture moved and took Troubles with him, much to Dad's relief!
How funny! I wish we could all put our Troubles in a pasture and be
done with them! But I digress, so let's continue with Balaam and his
talkative donkey.

There's so many twists and turns in this story that I don't
have the space here to share it all. In a nutshell, the story is about a
man named Balaam, who was being asked by King Balak (don't you
just love these names?) to go to the Israelites and curse them. After a
couple of discussions between the King, Balaam, and God, Balaam
saddled up his donkey and away he went. But then the trouble started. On the way, his trusted donkey strayed from the path Balaam
wanted to be on and went into a field. Balaam got the donkey back
on track, and they were now traveling on a narrow path between
two vineyards, with walls on both sides. And what did that donkey
do? She pushed herself up against the wall, crushing Balaam's foot!
Later, they were on another narrow path, but this time there was no
room to turn, so the donkey decided to just plop right down on the
path, with Balaam still riding her. Each time the donkey "misbe-

haved," Balaam would strike her. And here's where it gets even more interesting, and where the above scripture comes in…

The Lord actually caused the donkey to speak, and she asked Balaam what she had done to make him beat her three times. The next verse tells us that Balaam answered her. He was mad and was ready to kill her on the spot for going off course three times.

So, why was Balaam's donkey acting so crazy? As it turns out, she had actually seen an angel of the Lord standing in her way with a drawn sword—all three times! I don't know about you, but if I saw an angel standing in my way with his sword lifted up, I'd be finding a better way to get where I was going—pronto!

God was opposing Balaam as he journeyed on, but only the donkey saw what needed to be done. Later, Balaam's eyes were opened, and he saw the angel for himself. The angel told Balaam that if the donkey had not turned away from him, he would have killed Balaam and instead saved the donkey! Why was the angel standing in Balaam's way? Because Balaam was on a destructive path (verse 32).

Have you ever plunged ahead with your own idea, good or bad, and God used people to stop you because you didn't see the big picture? Or maybe the truth came from someone you would regard as simple. It's easy to rely on our own decisions, isn't it? In fact, we can get in our own way! I don't know about you, but I think I need to pay better attention to my "donkeys!"

Your Legacy…

When you're faced with a decision, look around you. God may be placing someone in your path to help you out. Don't be afraid to listen to what they say. They just may save you a lot of time and hurt! And who wants wasted time and pain to be part of their legacy?

What Gifts?

As each of you has received a gift (a particular spiritual talent, a gracious divine endowment), employ it for one another as [befits] good trustees of God's many-sided grace—faithful stewards of the extremely diverse [powers and gifts granted to Christians by] unmerited favor.

(1 Peter 4:10, AMPC)

Each one should use whatever gift he has received to serve others, faithfully administering God's grace in its various forms.

(1 Peter 4:10, NIV)

Don't we all love a gift that comes in a shiny package, ready to be torn open? Mom was notorious for messing with her gifts. She'd gently shake them or try to peek to see what was inside—days before she was supposed to open them! She was so cute that it made us laugh. I've been told by my children that I may have adopted the same behavior. I don't know what they're talking about…

But this scripture is not about gifts in a package. It's about gifts that are given to us spiritually, by the Holy Spirit Himself. Whoa! Really? Yes, and scripture actually has quite a bit to say about it. If you need a little boost, go to 1 Corinthians 12:1-11; Ephesians 4:11; and Romans 12:6-8. There are also many study guides to help you understand what spiritual gifts are. And there are spiritual gifts assessments available to help you understand your spiritual make-up.

So, why do I bring this topic up? As a Christian, spiritual gifts are a major part of who we are. It's a special area in your life that will build others up in a way only the Spirit can do. For instance, one of the gifts is called Hospitality. This person has the ability to make everyone feel welcome in their home. They don't worry if their pillows are perfect on the couch when someone drops by unexpectantly. In fact, the house is not their concern. It's the people inside the house that are. When you visit a person with this gift, you'll immediately feel comfortable and taken care of. They want to know how you're doing, and if there's anything they can do for you. It's all about your welfare. Can they have a nicely decorated house as well? Sure! But the minute you walk through the door, their concern is you. Those with this gift also love to give lodging and food to those who need it—messy house or not!

I know what my gifts are, and I can assure you hospitality is not mine! Oh, I'm glad you're at my house, and I do want to know how you're doing, but you can bet if you ring my doorbell when I'm not expecting it, I'm immediately concerned about whether the bathroom is clean, and the clutter is picked up off the couch. I'm not proud of this fact, but I am thankful that I know what my gifts are, and I try to gravitate towards what I can do through the Holy Spirit! When that happens, God is given the credit, and the people served are blessed in a very special way.

Have you ever left a gift unwrapped? I'm guessing you haven't. So, what are you waiting for? Open those gifts and find out what's inside!

Your Legacy...

If you don't know your area of giftedness, I encourage you to find out. It will be an "Ah-hah!" moment for you. You'll understand why you're drawn to certain areas in your life, and why you seem to excel in them. Most importantly, you'll learn why people seem to be blessed when your gift is evident, and God will be given the credit.

Beauty in A Broken Bottle

Charm and grace are deceptive, and beauty is vain [because it is not lasting], but a woman who reverently and worshipfully fears the Lord, she shall be praised!

(Proverbs 31:30, AMPC)

I admit I don't like seeing the skin on my face sag a little (does anybody have some duct tape?), and other things going south. I get up in the morning and feel like my younger self, then I look in the mirror to find my mind was playing tricks on me. I've tried solutions in a bottle to help with "fine lines." It's all in vain. They're still there, ever hoping to become a deep ravine! My mother had it right. She just used a little Jergen's Lotion, and away she went. She had the softest skin on her face of anyone I've ever known. It was like kissing a baby.

Have you ever noticed as you watch TV or get online that you see countless ads about feeling or looking younger? The goal is to turn back time and always be young and beautiful. But what is "beauty that lasts?" It sure doesn't come from a bottle with broken promises!

Proverbs 31:10-31 is a famous section of the Bible, and you may have heard about it. It's called the "Wife of Noble Character." Let me tell you, she's a hard woman to measure up to! She is brave, works hard, and is a great wife. She cooks, and she's a smart business-woman. She's kind and helps the needy. And the list goes on. But *none* of the attributes listed speak about her outer beauty, except to say that it's fleeting and in vain! What really matters is what's on the inside, and what shape our character takes.

I wonder... What would happen if all the commercials and internet ads were about building our character instead of re-building what's on the outside?

Your Legacy...

Look at the clock and time how long you spend getting ready for the day (your make-up, hair, and clothing.) Then take the same amount of time reading and getting to know the wife of noble character. How does this change your opinion of what's important?

_____

_____

_____

_____

If you're really brave today: Replace your beauty time with reading about the Wife of Noble Character.

Get Moving!

She girds herself with strength [spiritual, mental and physical fitness for her God-given task] and makes her arms strong and firm.

(Proverbs 31:17, AMPC)

Oh, that Proverbs 31 woman is at it again! Here we go—are you ready? Exercise. Some of you may want to throw this book down right now, and I get that. We're all so busy, how can we eke out time to go work out? I'm talking to myself as well when I say, "It's important". Our spirits are housed in these things called bodies, and if that body isn't functioning well, the rest follows. We're tired all the time. We get depressed. We have no energy to do the things we used to do. Creativity goes down. We do more sitting than standing or moving around. It's easy to get into that pattern. Been there myself and I continue to fight it. So, don't be hard on yourself, just get off the couch and move! Then give yourself a pat on the back. It may not be much at first, but at least it's something! Don't allow yourself to hear Satan's words of *"It's too late for you,"* or *"You'll never continue this, so why try?"* Just tell Satan that he doesn't own your body or your mind, and to take a hike of his own!

Mom had exercises to do even when she was no longer very mobile. She sat in her chair and went through the round of leg exercises provided for her by a professional. And those exercises were imperative in keeping her legs strong enough so she could walk around the house.

So, if you are someone who cannot do vigorous exercises due to health reasons, I understand. But even if you're only able to sit there and lift your legs up and down, do it! I promise you that once you get into an exercise routine, your body will actually let you know when it's time to move. Sounds crazy, but it's true. And if a sweet little woman in her nineties can do that much, so can you!

Your Legacy...

Take just five minutes today and do some exercises. How about walking while standing in place? That's easy! Once you have that mastered, do another five minutes to-morrow, and so on. Starting small can help you win small battles, which will give you the confidence to keep going. Or, join a gym and get a trainer. Knowing that you have an appointment with a fitness trainer will help get you there (Hmm... I wonder how I know that?)

_____

_____

_____

_____

Who's My Brother?

Then the just and upright will answer Him, Lord, when did we see You hungry and gave You food, or thirsty and gave You something to drink? And when did we see You a stranger and welcomed and entertained You, or naked and clothed You? And when did we see You sick or in prison and came to visit You? And the King will reply to them, Truly, I tell you, in as far as you did it to one of the least [in the estimation of men] of these My brethren, you did it to Me. [Prov. 19:17.]

(Matthew 25:37-40, AMPC)

My father served in the Navy during World War II. And, as with all military families and spouses, my mother served in her own way at home. She worked for a valve plant called the Walworth Company. When the war hit, the plant started making artillery shells, and Mom was one of the secretaries for the plant. She did her part to help during the war, serving in her community as the need arose.

So, where do you and I serve in today's world? Where is it that we can help others, but in essence, serve Christ? Or, as Mom noted, in verse 40, the people served and, "Did it for Jesus." I like that.

You know, there are many non-profit organizations in my hometown where I could go to volunteer, and I'm sure it's the same where you live. Even small towns have people in need. Or how about at church? Many hands are needed to get the various jobs done. Can't get out and about to help with your hands? Then how about making a donation to a worthy cause?

No matter how we get involved, let's just get started, what do you say? We'll be blessed, and so will those we serve!

Your Legacy...

While you're at church, ask the volunteer coordinator what needs to be done. There's usually no end of needs in a church. Or look in your newspaper or talk to city council members and ask them what volunteer possibilities there are in your area. Do you have a friend or two that are involved in a volunteer position that you are also interested in? Ask them to help you get started. Whatever you decide to do, just dig in. Don't be afraid. You'll meet new friends along the way.

_____

_____

_____

_____

Marriage

"Don't let marriage deprive you of time with God." A note from Mom in 1 Corinthians 7.

First Corinthians 7 is the marriage vs. singleness chapter. In this chapter, one is not necessarily better than the other, although, the emphasis is on staying single. The reason? To be single meant you could spend more time with God because you had no distractions with a spouse. Mom wasn't saying that she didn't like to be married to Dad, she was reminding herself to leave time each day for God. And from the looks of her Bible, she lived that sentiment.

While we need to spend time with our spouses to continue our growth as couples, we also need to give God part of our day as well. And spending time with God will serve to increase our relationship with our spouses. It goes hand-in-hand.

Your Legacy...
Today's legacy builder is three-fold. First, make sure you've spent that all-important time with God. Second, take time to pray together, and third, go out on a date with your special someone!

_____

_____

_____

_____

So Many Before Us

Therefore then, since we are surrounded by so great a cloud of witnesses [who have borne testimony of the Truth], let us strip off and throw aside every encumbrance—unnecessary weight—and that sin which so readily (deftly and cleverly) clings to and entangles us, and let us run with patient endurance and steady and active persistence the appointed course of the race that is set before us.

(Hebrews 12:1, AMPC)

Therefore, since we are surrounded by such a great cloud of witnesses, let us throw off everything that hinders and the sin that so easily entangles, and let us run with perseverance the race marked out for us.

(Hebrews 12:1, NIV)

In the previous chapter in Hebrews, chapter 11, there are many people listed that were able to accomplish their jobs by faith alone. These weren't easy jobs, and some seemed humanly impossible! Then we get to chapter 12, verse 1, and we are told that these faith-filled people, and countless others, are rooting for us as we continue *our* race. Isn't that awesome? Can you just imagine it?

If you've ever been to a football game, you understand the meaning of a great multitude of people sitting in the bleachers, many up high and excited to cheer their team on. Now just imagine that you and I are down below in the field working hard to win even though we don't know what actions others will take. We just move forward in faith. It can be difficult. But we are surrounded by the people who are cheering for us and want us to win as well. They are the people who understand the game and have faith in us until the game is over. I love this visual because I can close my eyes when I'm struggling with a challenge in my life and hear the faith-filled people that have gone before me cheering so loud that I need earplugs!

We no longer have to feel alone or feel like we are the only ones who are following Jesus in what seems to be a very hard-hearted world. We have the company of countless people who are cheering for us and who have set the stage for us. They have given us the example to follow. And you know what? We are doing the same thing by living our faith out loud. Our children watch and learn. And their children will as well. What do you want your faith-walk to look like—what legacy do you want to hand down to your children and those around you?

I can genuinely say my mother persevered and ran her unique race for ninety-four years. That deserves some whooping and hand-clapping right here on this Earth! Can you imagine that? Well, if you can't, realize that you are—right now—doing the same thing! One day at a time.

Your Legacy...

Make this the most important time of your day today. Get in a quiet place and take a hard look at the faith steps you've taken so far. What is it that you want your family and friends to remember about you? Are there things that may need to be changed so that your building blocks of faith will help the next generation? Will those around you say that you persevered and ran your race in faith?

_____

_____

_____

_____

Life Is Hard, But God Is Good

[Prompted] by faith Rahab the prostitute was not destroyed along with those who refused to believe and obey, because she had received the spies in peace (without enmity) [Josh.2:1-21; 6:22-25.]

(Hebrews 11:31, AMPC)

By faith the prostitute Rahab, because she welcomed the spies, was not killed with those who were disobedient.

(Hebrews 11:31, NIV)

Do you remember the chapter on the "great cloud of witnesses"? Believe it or not, Rahab the prostitute is among those in that "cloud." That list is considered to be the "Who's Who" of those who built their lives on faith.

You may be thinking, *I thought everyone in the Bible was perfect, so how did a prostitute get on that list?* In fact, the Bible is *full* of imperfect people—humans like you and me—who messed up a lot but tried their best to follow God's commands. I love that so much! This makes God so relatable. Because God is not sitting on His throne waiting to strike someone with lightning. He's waiting for you and me to hear Him so that we have fulfilling lives that He has set out for us to do. He loves us, He knows we're human, and He is oh-so-patient with us! This is a good thing because I've messed up throughout my life even now, and I know I won't have a perfect life from here on out.

So here I am, just trying to do the best that I can with what God gives me to do, while having faith that He'll take my wrongs and use them for right! God can and does use anyone if they walk hand-in-hand with Him.

Think you've done something that makes you ineligible for God's work? Check this list out:

- Noah—got drunk (Genesis 9:20-21).
- Moses—didn't speak well (Exodus 4:10).
- Abraham—let men take his wife—twice—to be their wife (Genesis 12:12-20, Genesis 20:1-17).
- Rahab—a prostitute (Joshua 2:1-21; Joshua 6:22-25; Hebrews 11:31).
- David—an adulterer and murderer (II Samuel 11).
- Jonah—ran from God (Jonah 1:3).
- Saul—persecuted Christians and then later become Paul, a Christian himself (Acts 8:3).
- Job—lost everything (Job 1:6, 2:10).
- Peter—denied Christ three times (John 18:15-18, 18:25-27).
- The Disciples—fell asleep while praying, at a very critical time for Jesus (Matthew 26:40, 43).

And this list goes on! Don't you feel better now, knowing that God can use us no matter what we've done? And one more bit of information regarding Rahab... she's included in the lineage of Jesus (Matthew 1:5)!

Your Legacy...

If you are struggling with life issues that you just can't forgive yourself for, look at the list of people God used in spite of their challenges. Ask God to forgive you if needed. But don't stop there. Forgive yourself! Move FORWARD. Don't let the past dictate your future with God! Move on!

Epilogue

Whether you decide to read this book once or refer back to it, thanks for being a part of my small world. Things are always better when shared with friends, don't you think?

I also hope that you will be spurred on to find the important pieces of your family's legacy. Like me, they may be hidden in plain sight! My mother never talked about how much she read and made notes in her Bible. She just learned from it every day, and then did her best to live it. I'm sure she never thought it would come to mean so much to her husband, children, and grandchildren as it has, and that it may help others as well.

Mom, we miss you bunches, and the memories you've given us make us smile! We are all so blessed to have had you in our lives, and we'll see you again in heaven!

Thank you for reminding us that we don't just leave a legacy, we live it as well—every day of our lives.

About the Author

Cindy Tharp is married to her high school sweetheart, and a mother of two grown children. She has two grandchildren, emphasis on grand! She lives with her husband in South Texas, and together they enjoy sitting at the Gulf of Mexico, watching the wildlife around them.

Cindy graduated with a bachelor's degree in social work. Although she worked at non-profit organizations as a social worker, she has also had more unusual jobs, such as a mural painter, a reporter for several small newspapers, owned her own photography business, and designed Bible studies—all the while serving as a pastor's wife for thirty of those years. She likes to knit in her spare time and enjoys cooking healthy meals (and maybe eat some chocolate along the way!).

Cindy has had a love for writing since she was small, and is thankful to be blessed with this, her first book.

References

Merriam-Webster Contributors, 2019. "Definition of Vital." Merriam-Webster Dictionary. 30 January 2019. https://www.merriam-webster.com/dictionary/artificialintelligence.

CPSIA information can be obtained
at www.ICGtesting.com
Printed in the USA
LVHW051405270519

619135LV00019BC/1062/P